**Parviz Tanavoli**

# Tacheh of Chahar Mahal

Translated by

**Amin Neshati**

**Tacheh of Chahar Mahal**

First published in 1998 by Yassavoli Publications
Colour separation : Farayand-e Gouya
Lithography : Naqsh Afarin
Cover designer : Aydin Avajeghe
Printed and bound in the Islamic Republic of Iran
Printed by Soroush Printing house
Published and distributed by Yassavoli Publications:
Bazaarche Ketab, Enqelab Ave. 13146, Tehran, Iran.
Tel: (9821) 6461003 Fax: (9821) 6411913


ISBN: 964 - 306 - 068 - 3

**To my daughter Tandar**

**Photographers:**

Majid Ehteshami, Parviz Tanavoli,
Davood Sadeqsa, M.R. Baharnaz and
Afshin Bakhtiar

## Tacheh of Chahar Mahal

The tachehs of Chahar Mahal, appeared in the Tehran bazaar for the first time in 1991. Their appearance caused some surprise, because Chahar Mahal is well known. For several years the region has seen a traffic in rug dealers and traders, who often return with hands full of the varieties of textiles from Chahar Mahal. So how was it that they never took notice of these pieces? I have been involved with Chahar Mahal textiles for years myself and have traveled frequently to the region, but I had never seen this variety. As a rule, if such textiles were identified and brought to public attention by someone else, they must have found their way into people's hands or been written about-neither of which was the case.



To get to the bottom of this mystery, I made a visit to Chahar Mahal and found my answer there. It has been some two decades that plastic, *juval*-like containers have replaced and supplanted *tachehs.*

Every time a *tacheh* was taken out of circulation because of wear and tear, it was substituted with one of these plastic things instead of a new *tacheh,* which had been the method in the past. With the introduction of cheap plastic *tachehs*, the village folk contented themselves with the synthetic containers, preferring to spend their wool, thread, time and collective effort on producing floor covers. Thus, the making of *tachehs* was gradually phased out.

A large number of the available *tachehs* have emerged from nooks and crannies in warehouses and closets — and sometimes stables — of villagers. Had it not been for the commendable rural habit of never throwing anything away and patching fabrics to make floor spreads for themselves or *jols* for their animals, these would have been lost as well. The *tachehs* that still survive serve as reminders of an important group of textiles from Chahar Mahal. Some of the patterns and designs on these *tachehs* have not been seen in other Chahar Mahal textile. The patterns, exhibiting features common to their other textiles, are of the nature of prototypes and *vagirehs*. It would be no exaggeration to say that the essence of Bakhtiari rugs is distilled in these little pieces and that they epitomize Bakhtiari rug patterns and designs. Aside from and in addition to this, it is the mysterious connection between the *tacheh*, the prayer rug, and the shepherds' salt bag — as well as other evidence such as its relationship with local architecture — that has prompted me to write a piece solely about the *tacheh*. In this discussion I have attempted, wherever possible, to include examples of each design, with the intention of bringing to light the beauty and richness of a class of textiles from this region that was about to be buried under the dust of time.

The word *tacheh* is one of the few Persian words for tribal and rural containers. 'Ta' or 'tai' in Persian means "bale and "cheh" is the diminitive suffix; hence, *tacheh* means "little bale". Since this word is of ancient Persian origin and has Indo-European roots, more research is needed into the possibility of its being akin to the German 'Tasche', which also means bag or sack.

The presence of Perso-Germanic cognates — 'shekar' and Zucker, tabesh, Teppiche to name a few — has for long been of interest to linguists, and it is these shared words that have led to answers about the Aryan race and its movements and migrations to different lands. It is appropriate, therefore, to add the word 'tacheh' to the list of several hundred Perso-Germanic cognates.

Aside from the authenticity and age of the word 'tacheh', there are other special features pertaining to these containers that call for greater research. Among these are their pattern, design, weave and structure. The enumeration of each of these special features and their comparison and connection with other textiles and phenomena from Chahar Mahal reveals the depth of the inter-connectedness of these containers and their lands. I turn my attention first to their structure.

The *tacheh* is a fairly large container, about the size of the *juval* but somewhat thinner. Each *tacheh* is woven from a piece of fabric about 130 cm.×100 cm. and has an area of 1.30 square meters. Roughly a fifth of this area consists of pile weave, and the rest is weft-faced plain weave. The pile weave often consists of symmetrical knots generally on one level (symmetrical$^1$), but they can also be of the sy$^2$ and sy$^3$ types[1]. In the *gelim* section, some *tachehs* have weft-wrapped embellishments, and one can see other weaving structures. These are also specialties of the region,

1- A landscape from Chahar Mahal-e Bakhtiari

2- Loading two separate tacheh

and will be discussed later. The warps of the *tachehs* are often of wool and sometimes of cotton. The use of cotton became more common among the Chahar Mahal weavers in the 20th century; therefore, a number of later *tachehs* woven are with cotton warps.

*Tachehs* were always woven in pairs and in one piece (fig.4). A woven fabric of this kind has dimensions of roughly 260 cm.×100 cm. It resembles a small *gelim* with two pile-weave, salt-bag-shaped sides at its two ends (fig.3). This *gelim* can be cut and converted into two separate *tachehs* (fig.2) or folded and sewn from the middle to form a twin *tacheh* (fig.4). In that case, the woven *gelim* is folded both length-and breadth-wise and its two edges are sewn together. For reasons of durability, the imprints on the two ends of the *tacheh* have a special structure which, by virtue of the increase in the warps and the wrapping of extra wefts around them, makes the fabric stronger. This reinforcement also holds true for the upper and lower segments of the *tacheh*. The upper portion of the *tachehs* often consists of special end-wrapping which is created through employing extra warps and two sets of extra wefts of contrasting colors, producing an end result that resembles a barber's pole. The lower section, meanwhile, which is less visible, shows no particular color or design, and here the makers have contented themselves with simple end-wrapping, with the same color as the field.

The *tacheh* has the same use as the *juval*, that is, primarily for the storing and moving of wheat and barley. The *tachehs* are filled at harvest time with wheat or barley, loaded onto donkeys or mules in pairs and taken either to the mill to be ground or home to be stored. The up and down placement of twin *tachehs* on the beast of burden, while more difficult because of their weight, is compensated for by their ease of the balance they create (fig.4).

Ownership of *tachehs* among farmers depends on the size of their crop and yield. Those who have more *tachehs* obviously are better off economically, and for the most part store their wheat and flour in granaries in a corner of their house, where they also keep their *tachehs* in stacks. The poorer ones, meanwhile, stack their *tachehs* in a corner of the same room in which they live and therefore derive greater visual pleasure from them. With a view to the population of Chahar Mahal, one can surmise that in the more distant past hundreds and even thousands of *tachehs* were found in the region. What has remained of this number is no more than a drop in the bucket, perhaps not exceeding a few hundred. These are the product of the last hundred years or so.

The presence of a few dated *tachehs* provides a clue to the dating of others. A large number of the dated *tachehs* belong to the early to mid-twentieth century period. The date woven into *tacheh* no.1 marks its age possibly at more than a hundred years, thus placing it in the latter part of the last century. This *tacheh* is not the oldest specimen extant, and many of the undated *tachehs* seem older. Nonetheless, determining their exact age is no easy matter, and here one must rely on experience,

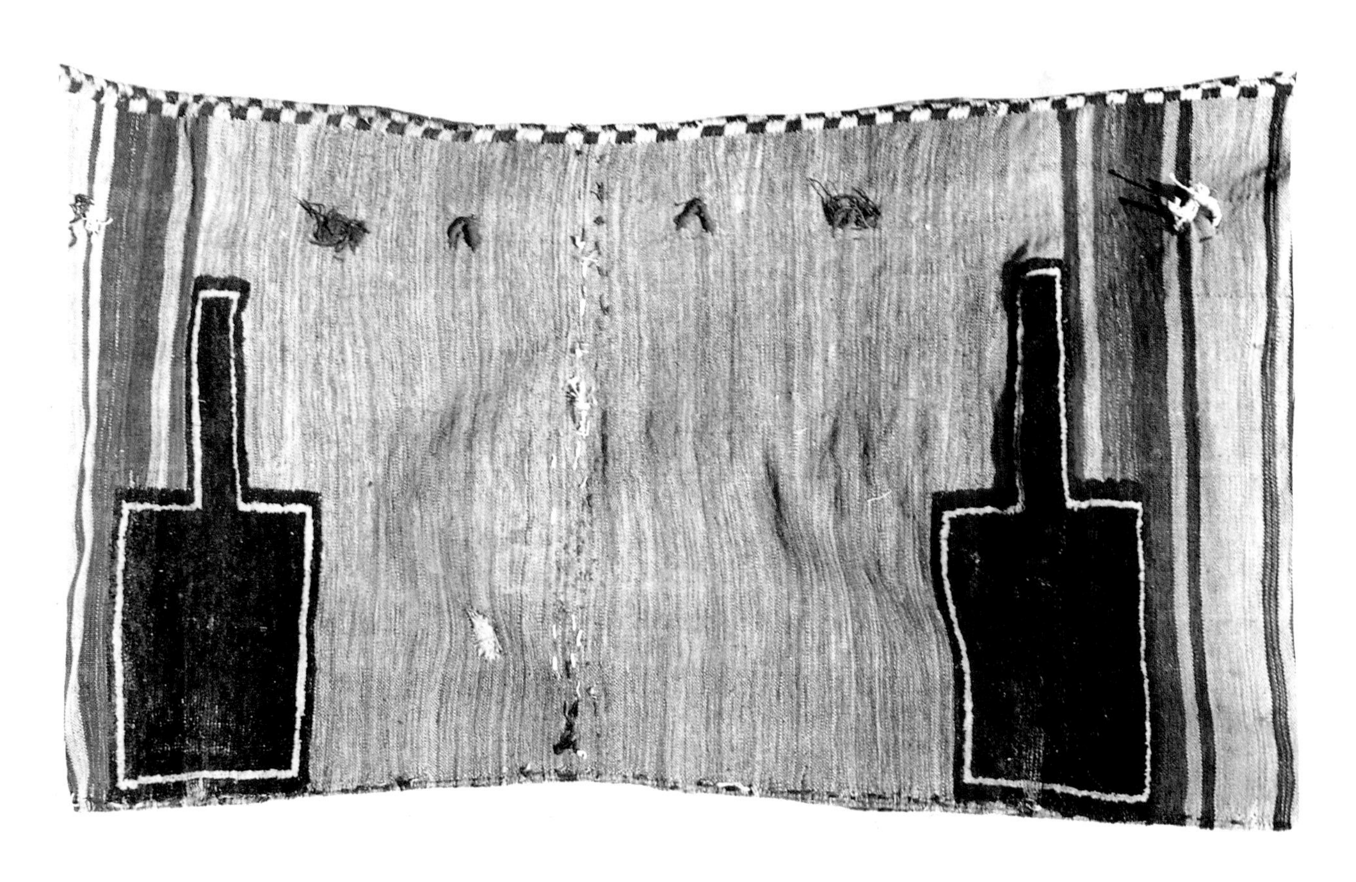

3- Twin tacheh, early 20th century

expertise and educated guesses. It would be no exaggeration to say that the age of some of the *tachehs* exceeds a hundred years, or more.

Chahar Mahal Bakhtiari, with an area 14,820 square kilometers, is one of the smallest provinces of Iran. By 1973 Chahar Mahal was considered a part of Esfahan province. In that year, it was elevated to provincial status by the central authority. Although this change was considered an important elevation in status so far as the division of the country was concerned, Chahar Mahal actually lost some area in geographical terms, inasmuch as previous to that year, and during the Pahlavi period (1925-1979), several portions of the extensive Bakhtiari lands were annexed to Khuzestan, Lurestan and Esfahan.

According to the census of 1976, the province held 903 inhabited and uninhabited villages, with a population of 400,000. The occupation of the majority of Chahar Mahal inhabitants is agriculture and animal husbandry. Rug-weaving has had a major role in the economic lives of the people from time immemorial. It is rare to find a village in Chahar Mahal where a rug loom has not been set up. Nevertheless, and despite the richness of the carpets of this area, very little has been done to promote their trade.

4- A pair of a twin tacheh on load

**Design and Pattern**

In terms of novelty of patterns and designs, Chahar Mahal Bakhtiari is one of the richest centers of rug-weaving in the country, so much so that this novelty can be felt from one village to the next, sometimes no more than a few kilometers apart.

In general, the body of textiles from Bakhtiari must be examined in two separate categories: the first, the textiles of the Bakhtiari Lors; the second, the products from Chahar Mahal. While these two groups are related tribally and ethnically, their lifestyles are not the same. Chahar Mahalis are villagers, living a rural lifestyle, while the Bakhtiari Lors are a nomadic people who spend half the year in Chahar Mahal and the other half in Khuzestan. The pieces they weave are different in many respects from the Chahar Mahal weaves. The making of pile rugs among the Lor tribes is considerably less common than flat-weaves. The reverse holds true for the Chahar Mahalis: the bulk of their products consists of pile rugs.

As far as patterns and designs are concerned, too, these two groups fall into separate categories. The patterns and designs of the majority of the Chahar Mahali textiles have their basis in soft lines and floral patterns, and one can easily see the imprint of the classical Persian rugs in them. The Lori textiles, on the other hand, have preserved their tribal purity. Nevertheless, despite these variations, there are several common features among the Chahar Mahal and Lori textiles, which I will indicate where appropriate.

The making of numerous and various containers is a necessity for nomadic tribes, and the Lors are no exception. The several varieties of *khorjin, khur, mafrash,* and salt bag[2], among others, are the handiwork of the nomadic Lors, in which the Chahar Mahalis have almost no part. The making of *tachehs*, however, is exclusive to Chahar Mahalis. Neither the Bakhtiari Lors nor any of their neighbors have any part to play in this area. However, the *tachehs* of Chahar Mahal on the one hand are influenced by the Chahar Mahal rugs, and on the other — to some extent — exhibit features of Lori textiles. Therefore, any recognition of *tachehs* must take into account these two categories of Chahar Mahal and Bakhtiari Lor textiles.



The *tachehs* of Chahar Mahal, despite their extensive variations in pattern and design, can be classified into three groups: first, the *tachehs* that are related to the *Gol Farang* rugs of Chahar Mahal, second, the *tachehs* that are inspired by the Lori *gabbehs*; and third, those created by a combination of the first two types. Of course, each of these groups are further classified into smaller categories, to which I will refer in their turn. But first I will turn to an analysis of the *Gol Farang tachehs* and the circumstances of the appearance of this design on rugs and *tachehs. Gol Farang* among the original and early patterns of Iran. Examples of it can be seen in several products from bygone eras, among them the textiles and ceramics of products from bygone eras, among them the textiles and ceramics of the seventeenth century and later [3]. However, further research is needed to determine how this Persian floral pattern got the name *Gol Farang* ("European flower"). The *Gol Farang* pattern consists of a rose in full bloom with its corolla. There is no end to the uses that Persian artists, among them the rug weavers of Chahar Mahal, have made of this pattern. Sometimes the flower alone is set in a frame and the repetition of the frames produces a square grid pattern which is called *qäb-e aineh* "mirror frame" (fig.6); at other times, a bunch of these flowers is placed on a rug in place of a central medalion, which is then called a *toranj-e Gol Farang, "Gol Farang* medallion" (fig.7). From another quarter, the very same method can be seen in the drawings on ceilings, in which the *Gol Farang* design has been worked in various ways (fig.8). It is entirely possible that the expression "mirror frame" has emerged from among the ceiling painters and artists of oil paintings.



The custom of painting ceilings is, as a rule, an ancient one, while the correspondence between floor rugs in a room and its ceiling is at least a few hundred years old. The ceilings that still remain from buildings in Qazvin, Esfahan, and Shiraz from the Safavid era and the seventeenth century onward all bear designs and patterns similar to the rugs of the period. Locating the rugs connected to these buildings and matching them with the extant ceilings is no easy task. These rugs are either dispersed or destroyed. In the Chahar Mahal region, however, it is still possible to find corresponding rugs and ceilings. This is because some of the buildings of the Bakhtiari *khans* are still standing and their rugs, woven at the behest

5- Detail of a tacheh with *gol farang* design

6- An oil painted wooden ceiling tile, late 19th century, 32×18 cm.

of their owners, have not been destroyed, although the bulk of them are in the hands of private collectors in the West. The correspondence of rug patterns and those on the ceiling, particularly in the reception room, was a sign of nobility in wealthy homes in Esfahan and Chahar Mahal, and possibly in other places as well. Practically every design and pattern woven into Bakhtiari rugs can be found on ceilings. These ceilings are for the most part made of oil-paint on wood. Painting on plaster was also common, but extant samples are far fewer than the wood ceilings, and most have been destroyed with the demolition of homes. The wood ceilings left over from these houses are still plentiful.



The basis for the composition of wood ceilings is akin to that of two groups of Bakhtiari rugs: one, lozenge and square-grid ceilings (*qab-e aineh*); the other, ceilings with *toranj*-like medallions. In both groups the same order and proportions are followed as in the borders and fields of Bakhtiari rugs. The salient common feature between the ceilings in both groups is the rose or *Gol Farang*, which appears in different patterns in the borders and the field of ceilings and rugs, except that on the ceilings the flower is accompanied by various birds. On some ceilings there are scenes depicting beautiful Western women or other European themes — a common practice in its day, but one out of the scope of our discussion. Suffice it to say that these pictorial scenes are not found in *Gol Farang* rugs.

The resemblances among Bakhtiari rugs, *tachehs*, and oil-painted ceilings with *Gol Farang* subjects provoke thought in the viewer and illustrate the circumstances of the mutual influences. The comparison of some of the *Gol Farang tachehs* with such ceilings and rugs is not devoid of pleasure. (For example, see figs 5 and 6 and nos. 1 and 2).

Before I discuss the second group of *tachehs* whose pattern is derived from the Bakhtiari *gabbehs*, I need first to describe these *gabbehs* briefly. Bakhtiari *gabbehs* came to the market about ten years after the *gabbehs* of Fars. Before the 1980 very little was known about them. If perchance samples came to light, they were labeled as Fars *gabbehs.* In the 1980 an extensive group of Bakhtiari *gabbehs* entered the market, thereby adding a new chapter to their numerous precursors on the varieties of rugs in Iran. Now one may confidently offer a separate class on the Bakhtiari *gabbehs*, for these are different from the Fars variety in many respects and it is appropriate for them to be introduced as an independent group.

What lies within the scope of this discussion are the patterns and designs of the Bakhtiari *gabbehs* and their connection with the *tachehs* of this region.

Practically every pattern that has been worked into the Bakhtiari *gabbehs* also appears in the *tachehs* of Chahar Mahal. It is noteworthy that the patterns and designs on the Bakhtiari *gabbehs* are fewer and more limited by far than those on their neighbors from Fars. Among the more prevalent of these patterns one must name the *kheshti*, square grid,

7- Bakhtiari rug with *gol farang* pattern, all wool, late 19th century, 207×137 cm. Private collection

8- Detail of an oil painted ceiling, late 19th century

checkered, multi-lozenge, pinstripe moharramat), and plain field types which are reproduced in *tachehs* also (nos. 6-28). The square-grid patterned *tachehs* have been designed along the same principles as the square-grid patterned *gabbehs*, meaning the area of the field is divided into squares that are colored in different ways, for instance alternating or striped (nos. 6 and 18).



There is another batch of these *tachehs* in which the same principle is followed, but the squares are considerably smaller. This pattern, better known as checkered, boasts fewer colors, and it is chiefly black and white or red and white that are used (nos. 3 and 13).

Pinstripe *tachehs* again are guided by the same principles as pinstripe *gabbehs*, i.e., the surface of the field is divided into diagonal or vertical lines (no. 9 and figs 11 and 12). Sometimes the stripes appear in toothed herring-bone (no. 28).

A considerable number of *tachehs* have a plain-field design. The prototype and origin of this design is taken from *sofrehs*[4] and also used extensively in *gabbehs*. In one batch of plain-field *tachehs* the words "Ya Ali" can be seen (nos. 20 and 21), the purpose being to remind one of the Imam Ali's name and to ask his assistance when lifting loads — a common enough practice. In some of these *tachehs* simplicity has reached its peak and even a border is dispensed with (no. 31). Aside from the patterns already mentioned, there are others found in *tachehs* which are of the nature of *gabbehs*,meaning they follow the same geometric system. The prototype for these has not been observed in Bakhtiari *gabbehs*, however. In some of these *tachehs* a herringbone design is employed (no. 22); others show no particular arrangement. For instance, in the simple background of *tachehs* number 33 there are two non-standard square patches of color. In *tachehs* number 37 the triple-lozenge arrangement is created by three color patches.

The third group of *tachehs* are those that are created from a combination of the last two groups. In other words, they are an amalgam of the various figures and floral designs in vogue in the Chahar Mahal rugs and Bakhtiari *gabbehs*. For this reason, in terms of number and variety they are the largest group and are classified into several smaller groups. The chief pattern for one of these subgroups is the rosette, which appears in some in the form of a single medallion (no. 40) and in others in a group (no. 41) The *tachehs* generally have a plain homogeneous background and a narrow border, and sometimes they have no border at all (no. 40).

There is another category of these *tachehs* whose field design is made up of the repetition of smaller flowers. The famous *boteh* design (no. 42) or spherical flowers can be seen in these *tachehs* (nos. 43-47). In one group of *tachehs*, there is an effort to show a tree with many branches, but since the work space is limited, the tree has turned into several wishbone shapes clustered atop of one another (no. 50).

Finally comes the group which is formed by the elements referred to above: the design is sometimes a blend of the *Gol Farang* with a

9- Bakhtiari gabbeh, Neiriz Gallery, Berlin

10- Detail of tacheh no. 11 with square grid design

multi-petaled flower (no. 56), sometimes a herringbone pinstripe alongside repeated instances of the *boteh* (no. 48), and sometimes a combination of the *Gol Farang,* rosette, and the multi-limbed shrub. There are other designs also (nos. 58 and 59). Occasionally there exist some *tachehs* in which their pile section differs from the ordinary *tachehs* (no. 60).

**Weaving Centers**

Determining the location where the Chahar Mahal *tachehs* were woven is not easy. As mentioned earlier, until the not-so-distant past *tachehs*-weaving flourished in all the villages of Chahar Mahal. However, the hiatus in *tachehs* weaving in the last two decades broke the chain of continuity. With the discovery of the *tacheh* in recent years and the ensuing rush of buyers, the villages that held these articles were soon stripped of them, and no records were kept. Thus, the task of determining a *tacheh's* village of origin has been rendered difficult. Nonetheless, Chahar Mahal *tachehs* can be classified into five groups based on their common features; each group covers an extensive area of the Chahar Mahal region and embraces several villages. So far as rug-weaving in Chahar Mahal is concerned, these five territories enjoy greater fame than other areas and their names are well known to insiders in the rug trade. In each case the area's radius extends a long way. Insofar as all of them taken together comprise the entire area of the Chahar Mahal territory, they are:

1) Shahr-e Kord, Chalshotor, and Saman

2) Chadegan and the northern villages

3) The central villages

4) The south

5) The west

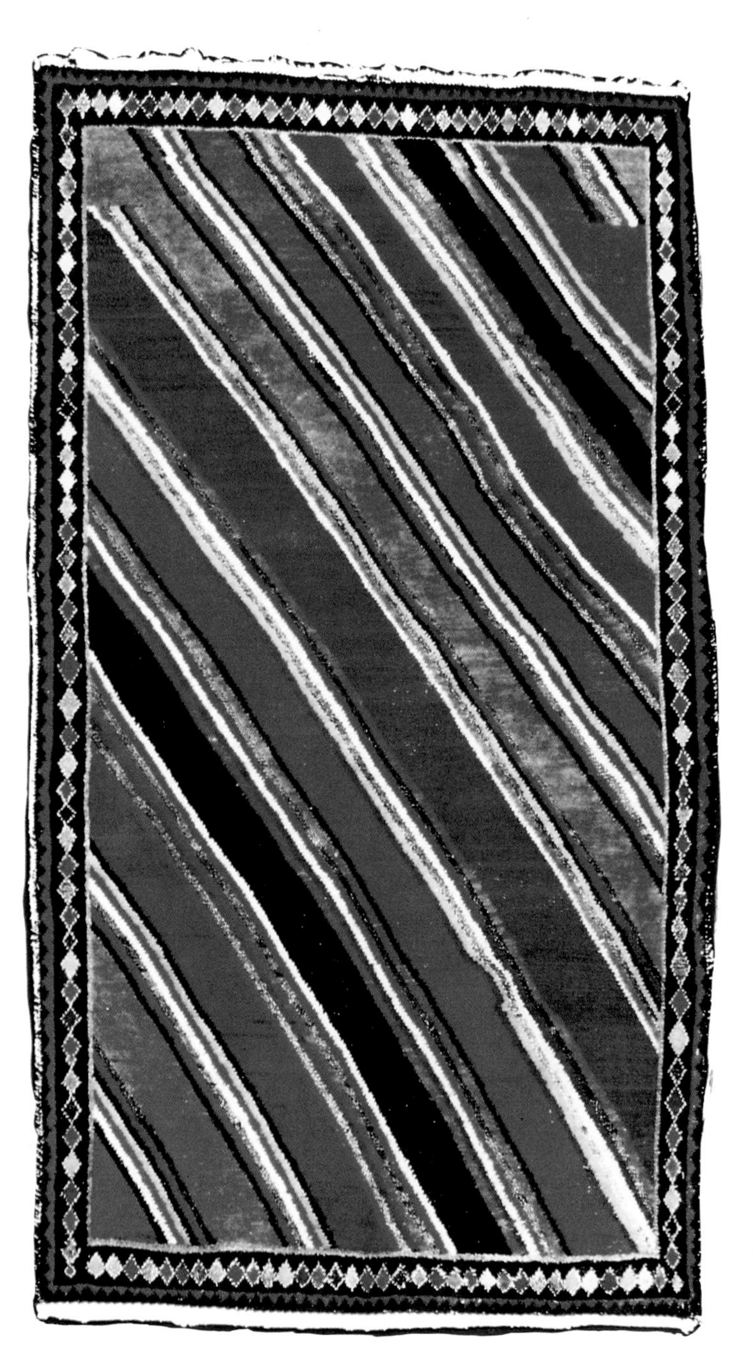

11- Farsi gabbeh, Neiriz Gallery, Berlin

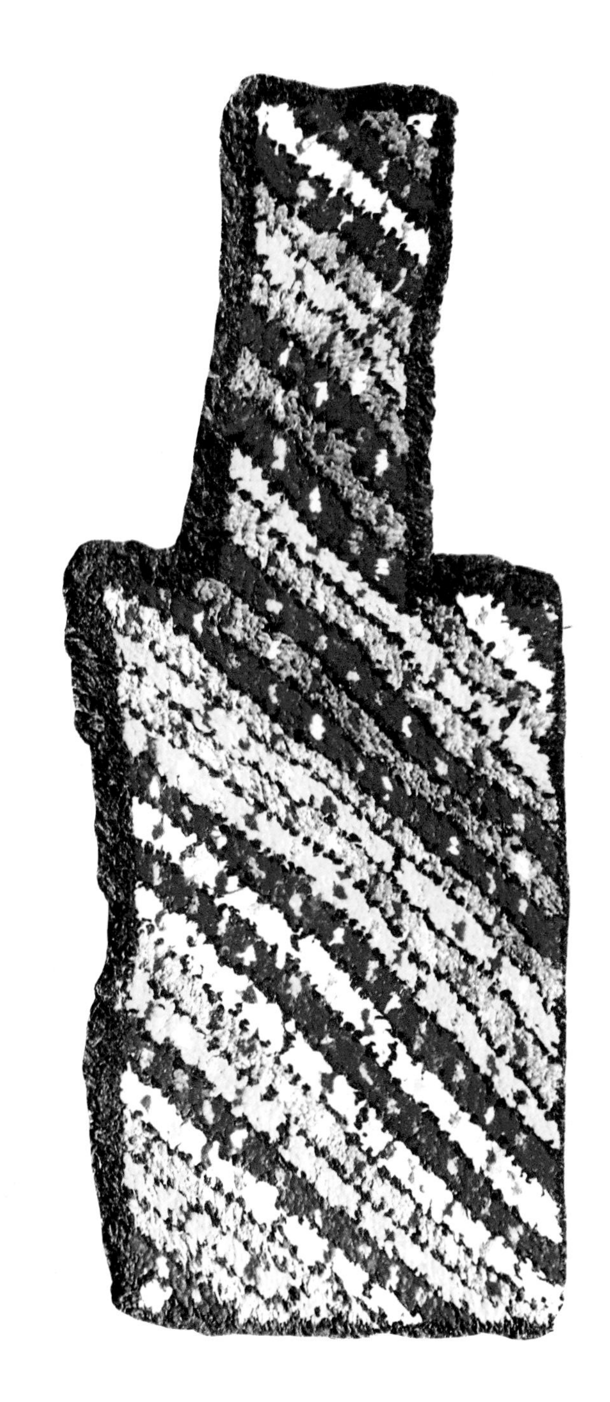

12- Detail of tacheh with pinstripe design, 184×105 cm.

Shahr-e Kord, Chalshotor, and Saman: The seat of Chahar Mahal, Shahr-e Kord, is now a big city with a large population. Not too long ago it went by the name of Deh Kord (Kord Village), and life there was no different from the other villages in the area. Its textiles enjoyed a considerable reputation, and it is likely that some of the rugs and *tachehs* attributed to Saman and Chalshotor were actually produced in Shahr-e Kord. Saman and Chalshotor are a few kilometers from Shahr-e Kord and constitute the most important of the centers of rug-weaving in Chahar Mahal. The overall reputation of the rugs of Chalshotor and Saman is owing to the delicate and fine workmanship which has gone into executing their designs and which, from ages past, has rendered them of great value. Aside from their workmanship, the rugs of Saman and Chalshotor bear the well-established and well-known designs that one might call classic designs of Chahar Mahal. These can also be seen in the *tachehs* associated with Saman and Chalshotor, which boast fine execution and a delicate and compact weave. The field in the majority of Chalshotor and Saman *tachehs* is dark blue, sometimes plain and homogeneous (no. 21) and sometimes embellished with a variety of *Gol Farang* sprays (nos. 2 and 53) or geometric medallions (no. 9). All of them have narrow borders constituted of various colors. The *gelim* section in the *tachehs* of Saman and Chalshotor is woven more tautly than in others made elsewhere, and in some of its stripes it is employed with an alternating weft-faced plain weave with two constrasting colors.

Chadegan and the northern villages: Chadegan is one of the northern villages of Chahar Mahal and sprang into being on the shores of the beautiful lake recently created by the Zayandeh-rud Dam. Chadegan and its surrounding villages are an important center of rug-weaving. The rugs woven here demonstrate greater freedom of execution, and the meticulousness of the rugs of Chalshotor is relaxed here. The *tachehs* of Chadegan are also more varied in terms of pattern and design, but their coloration lacks the brilliance and sparkle of Chalshotor and Saman rugs and seems more muted. Brown is often color of choice for the field. Among the more common patterns here is the rosette, sometimes executed once and sometimes repeatedly (nos. 36 and 41).



The central villages: Among the most productive areas, the central and villages yield the most diverse varieties of *tachehs* and rugs. In the ten-odd villages between Gandoman and Farsan, one can find numerous rug-like products, among them *tachehs.* In these villages, several forms of the *Gol Farang* pattern and *Gol Farang* combination patterns are produced, as are patterns on *gabbehs.* These are very colorful, and one sees lively colors — pink, bright green, purple, russet yellow — in the designs. One of the peculiarities of a group of these *tachehs* is their upper end: unlike most *tachehs*, in which this part is wrapped in barber-pole designs in two contrasting colors (namely, black and white), here it is plain and of the same color as the field (nos. 2 and 5). Among the villages that have

◀ 13- Bazoft village in Chahar Mahal

made the most significant contributions to *tacheh*-weaving, Sefid Dasht and Faradbonbeh must be mentioned.

The south: There is a group of *tachehs* produced here that share certain features in their weave, pattern, and coloration. The pile-weave bodies of these *tachehs* are smaller, and their necks longer, than those of *tachehs* from other areas. Fewer colors have been used in their weave, chiefly blue and white, and several have checkered or zigzag patterns. In a few, there are other colors used between the blue and the white. As far as structure, too, they are different from other *tachehs*. On these *tachehs* there is a considerable amount of weft wrapping that extends in a column from the neck and immediately follows the pile weave (nos. 3,9 and 13). Similarly, a few of them have a weft-wrapped band of two contrasting colors (nos. 9 and 13). Though the exact production center of these *tachehs* has not been determined as yet, we have some idea of the range. They are possibly from the southwestern villages of Chahar Mahal and the region of Lordegan.



5) The west and the Bazoft valley: The *tachehs* made here, which I consider the most interesting and creative, have geometric and *gabbeh*-like patterns for the most part, or have been woven with extreme simplicity. My efforts at finding the production center of these *tachehs*, I must admit, have not met with success. Older residents and experts in Chahar Mahal

consider them the work of mountain dwellers and attribute them primarily to the northwest, such as the villages around Shurab or the villages in the Bazoft valley. However, inasmuch as *tacheh* weaving has been suspended for some time, verifying this claim is beyond the realm of possibility. It is not improbable that these *tachehs* were made by the Bakhtiaris living on the other side of Zardkuh and other villages nearby. The designs on some of the *gabbehs* found in this area are similar to these *tachehs.* Among them are the lozenge and zigzag *tachehs* (nos. 22 and 26). Likewise, it is not unreasonable to attribute to mountain dwellers, who enjoy less access to the various colors, some very simple — albeit attractive — *tachehs* (nos. 22 and 23).



**Symbolism**

Now that a description of the *tacheh* weaving area and of the circumstances of their use has been given, it would not be inappropriate also to examine the circumstances of the creation of their designs and their aesthetic value. The object of this review principally is to examine that part of the *tacheh* that resembles a salt bag and consists of pile weave. Although this section comprises roughly one-fifth of any *tacheh*, it is nonetheless the most important part — the heart and soul of the *tacheh*, so to speak. It is true that the Bakhtiaris weave their containers in the two structures of flat-weave and pile weave, and a *tacheh* is nothing other than a container. But in a sense there is a difference between *tachehs* and other

Bakhtiari containers — *khurs, khorjins,* and salt bags — with respect to their utilitarian or non-utilitarian natures.

The pile-weave portion of the Bakhtiari *khorjins* and salt bags is situated at the bottom of the container, the purpose being to prevent abrasion[5], for it is this very bottom section that touches the ground constantly, therefore experiencing greater wear than the other parts. This explains why the pile-weave portion of these containers is woven thick and coarse and its patterns and designs, wherein the maker has contented herself with repeating some of the figures that appear in the field, are of secondary importance. The reverse is true for *tachehs*, i. e., the pile-weave portion comprises the body of the *tacheh* and is its exterior, at its most visible when the *tacheh* is full. It is not woven to prevent abrasion, but is solely for show and beauty. Why this portion is woven in the shape of shepherds' salt bags is a question that requires extensive research. Here we will point to few of the problems that might have bearing on its creation. It is altogether likely that there are other aspects to this riddle that have not suggested themselves to this writer.

The pile-weave portion of a *tacheh* resembles a salt bag so closely that it is sometimes imagined that a pile-weave salt bag has been sewn over a piece of *gelim.* A discussion of the making of the salt bags, as well as their size and shape, appeared earlier in my book *Nan va namak* (Bread and Salt), and therefore needs no repetition here[6]. But a recapitulation of the major concepts is necessary for a continuation of this discussion. As mentioned

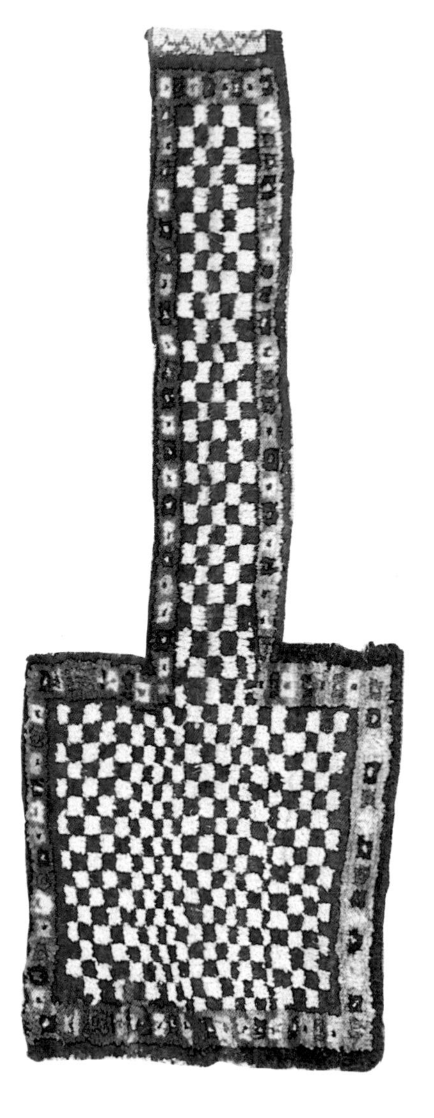

14- Pigeon tower, in Najafabad orchard, 15- Detail of a checkered design tacheh, early 20th century

16- Inside a pigeon tower, near Esfahan

earlier, the shape of shepherds' salt bags is not unrelated to prayer or *mehrab* rugs.

Several views have by now been put forth concerning the circumstances of the appearance of this design on rugs. Many have considered it a replication of the appearance of animal skins, which were the first human floor spreads. Others have gone a step further and compared it to the entrances to caves in which early man lived[7]. If we consider even minutely the notion by Stephanie Dalley that man's/woman's beliefs in early civilization benefited from a patchwork of beliefs or, in today's terminology, anaclectic amalgam, and that he/she often sewed a tiger skin (or that of other animals) onto his/her felt floor spread[8], then accepting the hypothesis of the salt bag with the appearance of an altar sewn onto a flour *juval* may become easier, especially since a relatively large group of *tachehs* is comprised of those with leopard-and tiger-and leopard — like patterns, such as zigzag and pinstripe or cintamani[9]. Certainly, behind all these suppositions there is an element of truth, and such a fundamental design has roots older than the *mehrabs* in mosques. But one can not dismiss the truth that *mehrab* rugs and their patterns reached their zenith in Islamic civilisation and culture. This design has a strong resemblance to shepherds' salt bags, particularly in tribal and rural rugs, among them Baluchi prayer rugs (fig.18). The design of these rugs, similar to shepherds' salt bags, is composed of two parts: the body and the neck. The body is the portion where the supplicant sits and rises, while the neck is where she/he lays her/his head in prostration. The reason the form of prayer rugs has been chosen for shepherds' salt bags is the reverence and sanctity attached to salt among Muslims and especially Iranian. The transfer of this form onto *tachehs*, meanwhile, is not unrelated to the relationship between bread and salt, insofar as *tachehs* served as repositories for wheat, barley, and flour — the raw material for bread. It appears in the *mehrabs* of mosques and other holy places and even on the illuminated pages of religious texts — in other words, wherever the presence of God or his bounties is felt. In short, it has become a "sacred symbol". Inasmuch as this headless torso is used in shepherds' salt bags (and, of course, it serves to prevent the spillage of salt), its presence on *tachehs* is akin to a seal of sanctity. It signifies that the container holds wheat, barley, or the flour made from them, and must be handled with care so that the grains do not spill underfoot where they might be subject to disrespect. By equating these twin bounties of God, the *Chahar Mahal* custom of producing containers for the stuff of bread (flour and wheat) in the form of a salt container is ingenious enough to arouse wonder. Weaving large receptacles for wheat and flour in the likeness of a salt bag might have translated inner beliefs into tangible reality directly, but it would not produce a practical or utilitarian container. Instead, the weaver made a large container with a wide opening and worked the sacred symbol into it, thereby achieving both objectives. Another factor that influenced the appearance of *tachehs* was the pigeon

17- Salt Bag, Afshars of Varamin, mid-19th century, 56×38 cm. Private collection

18- Baluchi prayer rug, late 19th century, 122×78 cm. Private collection

tower. The pigeon tower has an appearance similar to the salt bag or the pile-weave portion of the *tacheh*. This means that it, too, is comprised of a body and a neck; of course, in the pigeon tower this structure is three-dimensional. Until very recently, there were one or several pigeon towers in every farm or orchard in the villages of Esfahan and Chahar Mahal (fig.14). These towers were made as nests for the wild pigeons, the intention being to use the manure from the birds for fertilizer. Esfahani ingenuity created these towers to answer the need for manure in agriculture[10]. Wild pigeons entered the tower through the holes in the upper part and made their nests. The interior structure of the tower was contrived with intelligent calculations consisting of the forward or backward position of lozenges (fig.16), creating hundreds of nests for pigeons. The nests were built such that the waste from the birds dropped to the bottom of the tower. The farmer or owner of the tower then collected the waste every so often and used it in planting. It seems pigeon manure was considered the best kind for agriculture.



The bodies of some of the towers bear several necks instead of a single one. These towers belonged to the khans who owned larger farms and orchards[11].Towers belonging to villagers were generally fairly narrow cylinders, with the necks narrower still. In terms of proportion, they are closer to *tachehs* with the very checkered pattern that is created on the bodies and necks (fig. 16).

The pile-weave or salt-bag portion of every *tacheh* has a field and border. This salt-bag-like "rug" rests on a coarsely woven *gelim* background; that is, both have been woven into and blended in with each other. Unlike the multicolored *tachehs* themselves, the backgrounds have earthen colors, and generally undyed brown or beige wool is used in them. The blending of these two weaves and the contrast between their coloration cannot be unintentional. Some of them remind one of a flower growing in the desert, while others evoke a glittering gemstone ring in the midst of smoldering ashes.

19- A Bakhtiari family migrating

## NOTES

1- For more information on these structures see: Parviz Tanavoli, Kings, Heroes and Lovers: Pictorial Rugs from the Tribes and Villages of Iran. London, 1994, p. 64 f.

2- For variety of Lors of Bakhtiari containers see: Amadeo de Franchis and John T. Wertime, Lori and Bakhtiari Flat-Weaves, Tehran, 1976, pp. 34-109.

3- Carol Bier, ed., Woven from the Soul, Spun from the Heart, Washington D.C., 1987, pp. 175-177

4- Parviz Tanavoli, Bread and Salt: Iranian Tribal Spreads and Salt Bags, Tehran, 1991, pls. 5,6 16 and 30-33

5- Ibid

6- Op. cit. (4) p. 39 f.

7- James Mellaart, et al., The Goddess from Anatolia, vol. III, Milan, 1989.

8- Stephanie Dalley, "Ancient Assyrian Textiles and the Origins of Carpet Design" Iran: Journal of Persian Studies, no. , London,  ,pp. 117-134

9- Gerard Paquin "Cintamani" Hali: The International Magazine of Fine Carpets and Textiles, issue 64, London, 1992

10- Morteza Farhadi, "Nim Negahi be Kabutar Khaneha-ye Iran" (a look at the Pigeon Houses of Iran), Iran Zamin, nos. 4 and 5, 1372/1993, pp. 40-53.

11- Roland Rainer, Traditional Building in Iran, Gratz, 1977, p. 139.

12- Op. cit. (4) p. 21 f.

1 - 117 *x* 87 cm.

2 - 132 *x* 100 cm.

3 - 101 *x* 98 cm.

4,5 - 115 *x* 71 cm.

6 - 225 *x* 92 cm.

7,8 - 113 *x* 103 cm.

9 - 105 *x* 123 cm.

10 - 105 *x* 123 cm.

11,12 - 132 *x* 106 cm.

13 - 117 *x* 56 cm.

14 - 140 *x* 105 cm.

15,16 - 103 *x* 68 cm.

17 - 278 *x* 90 cm.

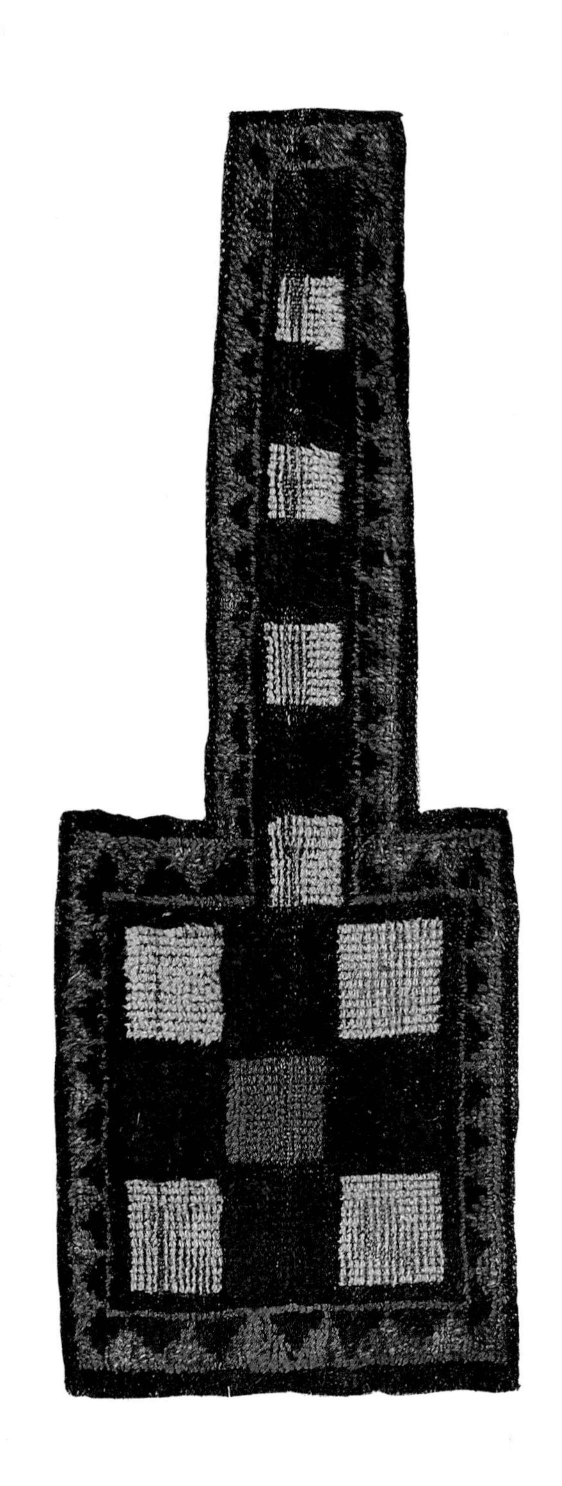

18,19 - 97 *x* 87 cm.

20 - 100 *x* 100 cm.

21 - 133 *x* 106 cm.

22,23 - 111 *x* 57 cm.

24 - 103 *x* 103 cm.

25 - 100 *x* 82 cm.

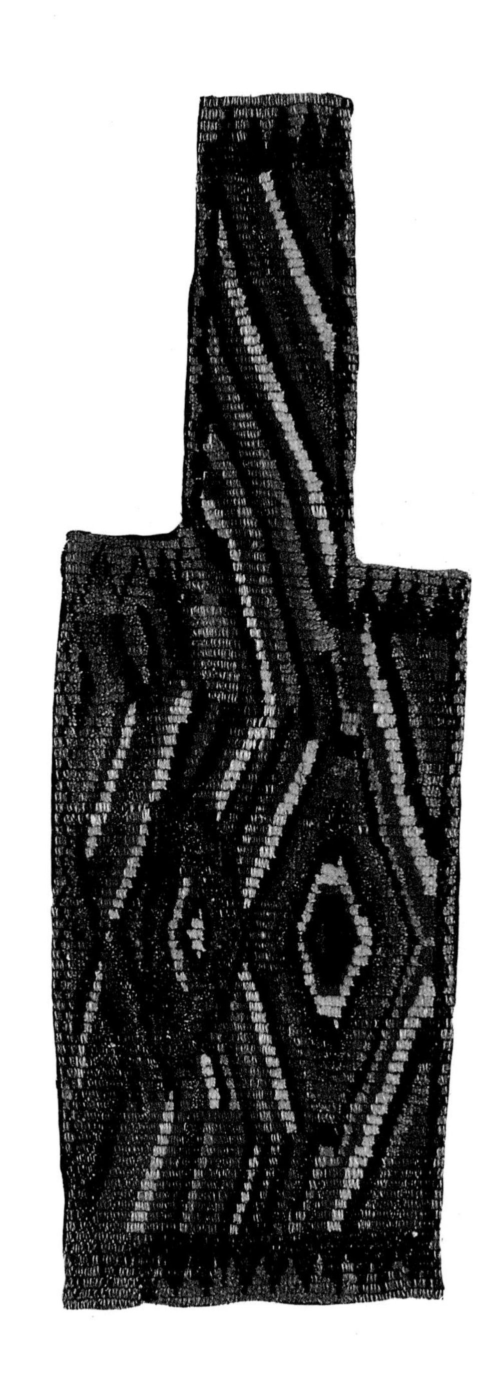

26,27 - 83 *x* 62 cm.

28 - 270 *x* 104 cm.

29,30 - 119 *x* 126 cm.

31 - 123 *x* 100 cm.

32 - 90 *x* 81 cm.

33,34 - 114 *x* 134 cm.

35 - 135 *x* 103 cm.

36 - 105 *x* 112 cm.

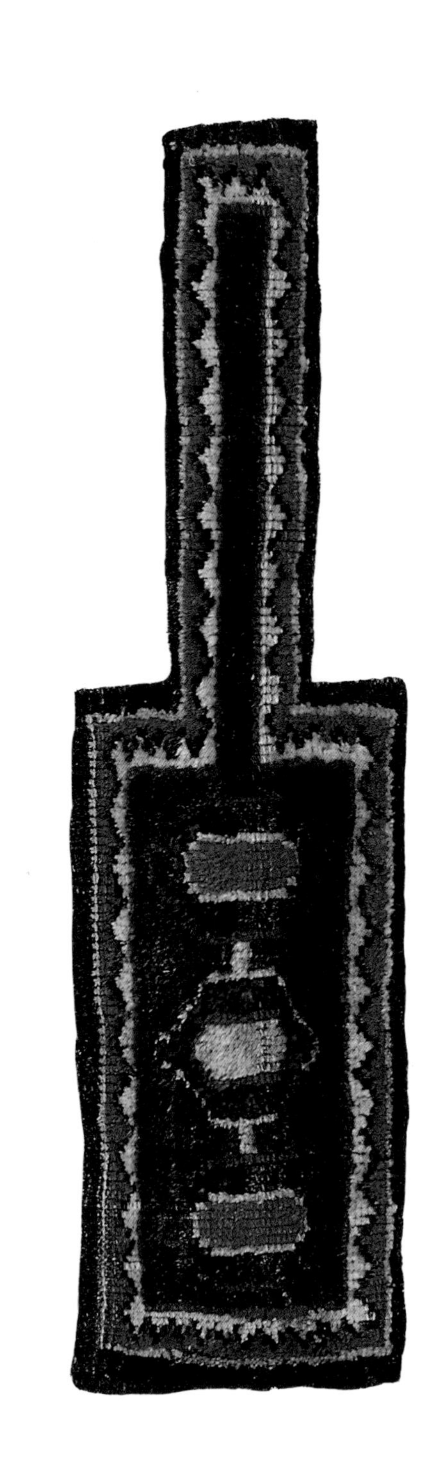

37,38 - 85 *x* 93 cm.

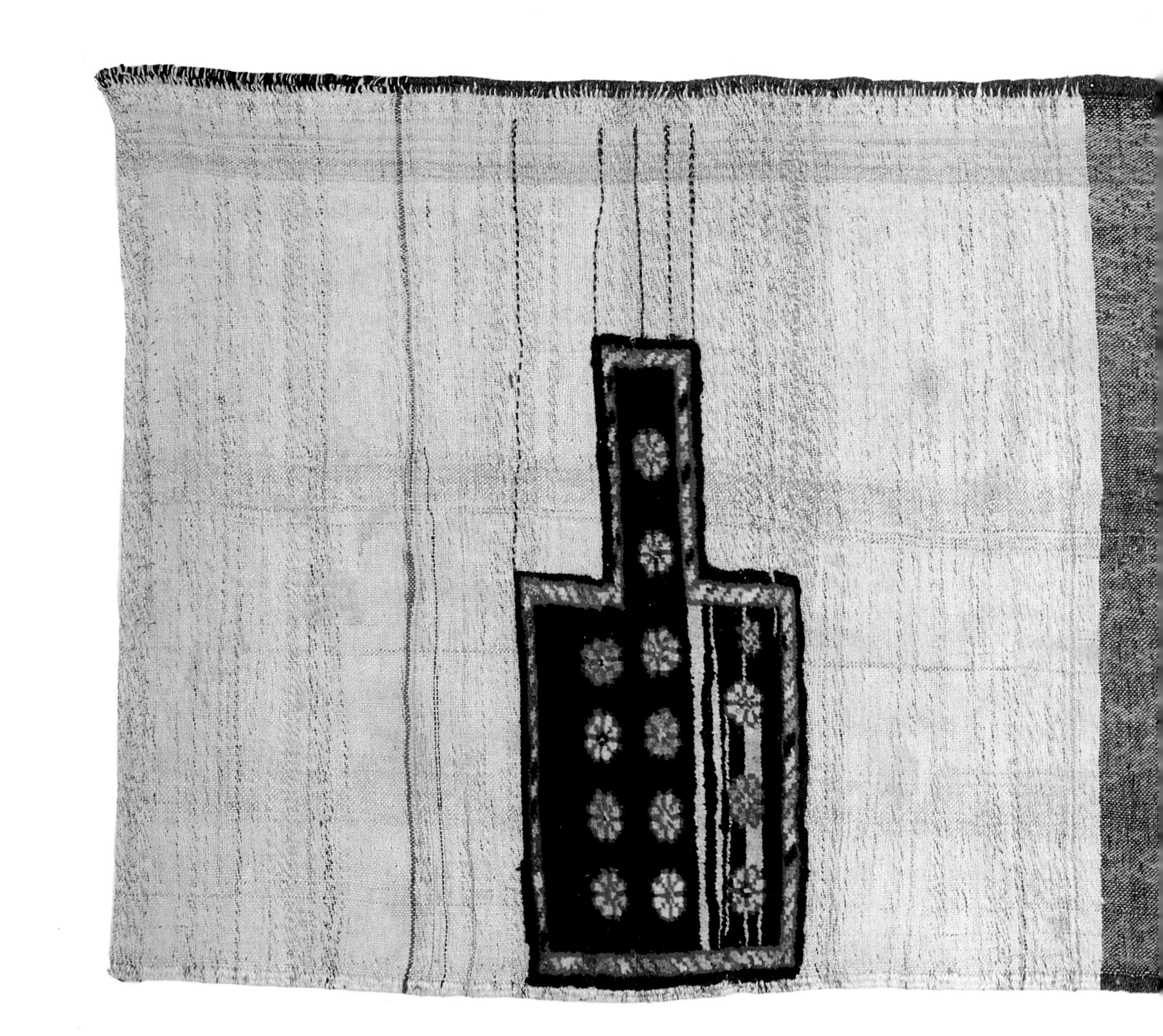

39 - 239 *x* 95 cm.

40 - 113 *x* 87 cm.

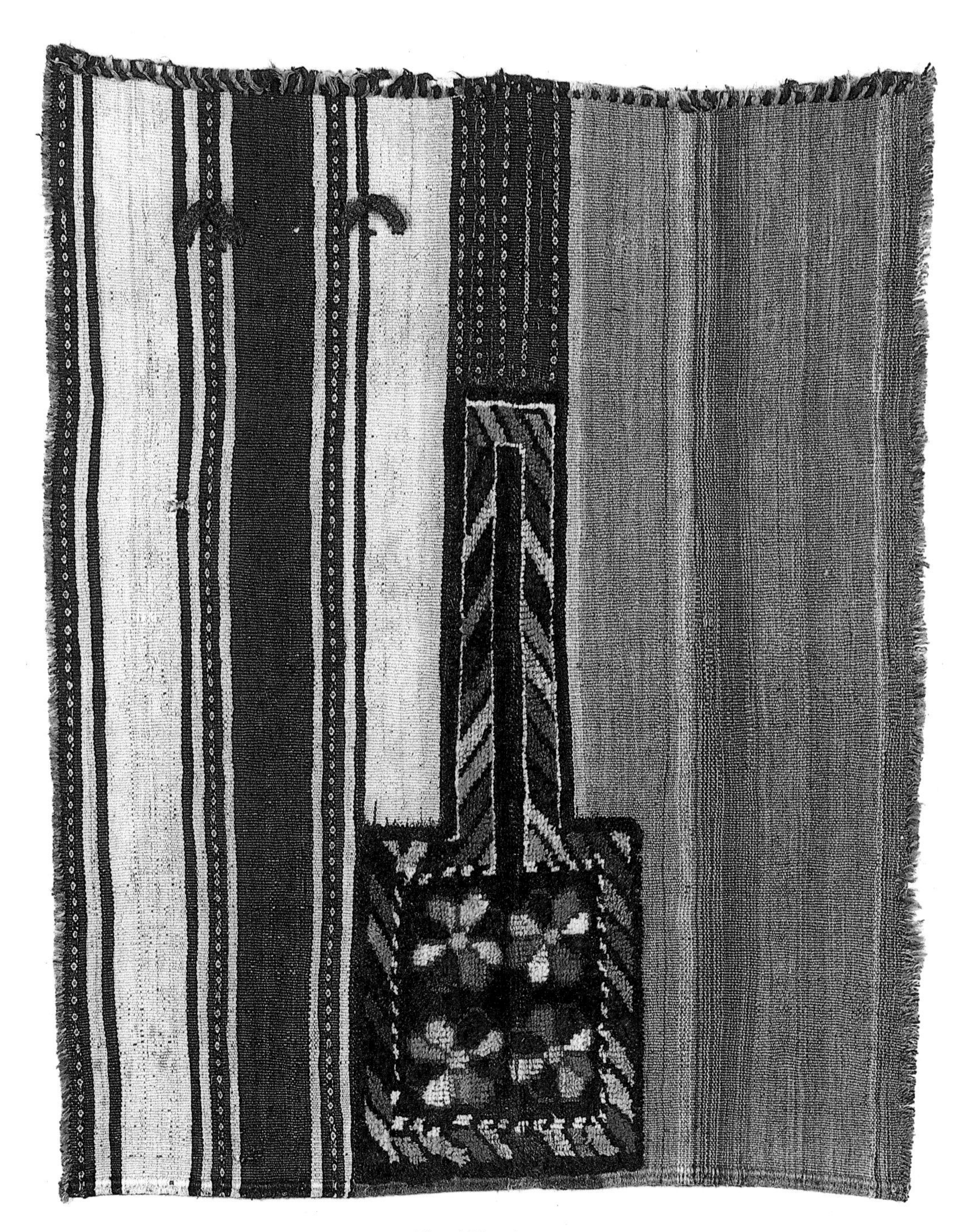

41 - 100 *x* 81 cm.

42 - 89 *x* 92 cm.

43 - 95 *x* 115 cm.

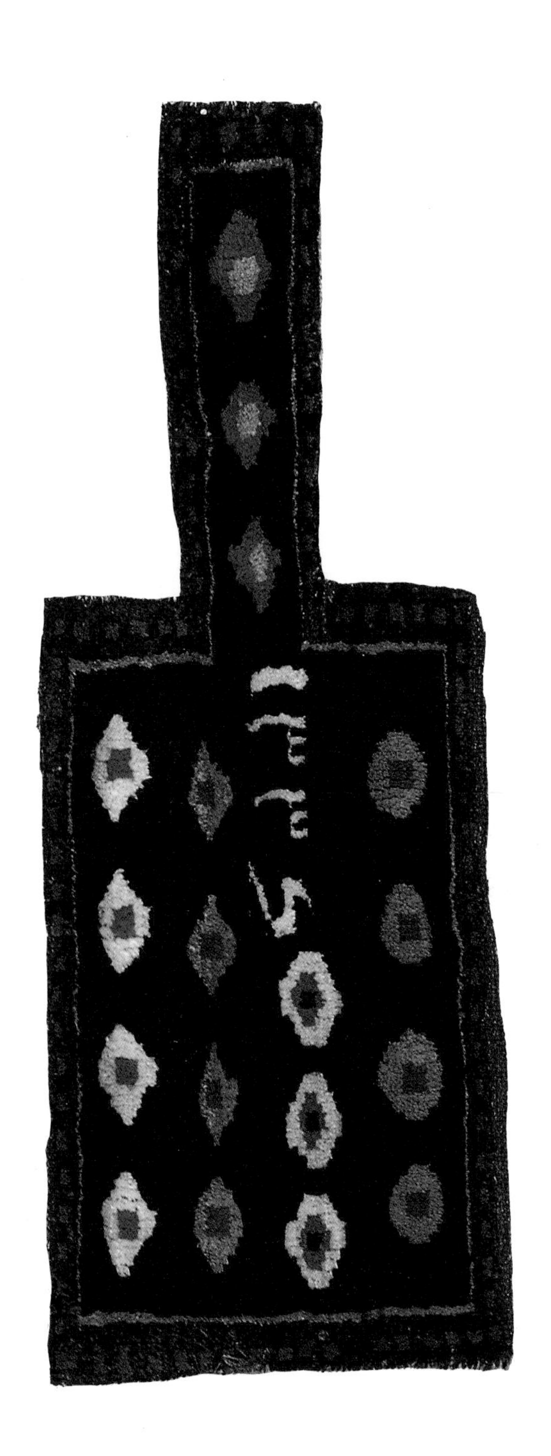

44,45 - 112 *x* 114 cm.

46,47 - 89 *x* 74 cm.

48,49 - 116 *x* 114 cm.

50,51 - 115 *x* 93 cm.

52 - 96 *x* 47 cm.

53 - 106 *x* 66 cm.

54,55 - 84 *x* 59 cm.

56,57 - 95 *x* 92 cm.

58 - 110 *x* 116 cm.

59 - 95 *x* 102 cm.

60 - 112 *x* 243 cm.